The Myth of the Vertical Stripe

Poems for women of a certain age

By

Ellie Wilkie

The Myth of the Vertical Stripe

Ellie Wilkie

Printed and bound in Australia

by Fineline print and copy service Perth WA

ISBN – 0-646-46943-6

Contents

All women will be familiar with the fiction purveyed by women's magazine fashion editors that vertical stripes make one look thinner.

If only!

Wear horizontal and enjoy it, I say.

The
Myth of the Vertical Stripe

I'm feeling good. I feel a winner.

Vertical stripes make me look thinner.

And even tho' I've had my dinner,

I'm confident I'm looking slimmer.

I read it in a magazine article,

If you too are rounded wear the vertical.

I'm feeling gorgeous. I'm looking great.

These stripes so completely change my shape.

You rounded ladies can surely see,

With well placed stripes you could look like me.

You too could be a sexy winner

Vertical stripes make one look thinner.

A woman of a certain age

As a woman of a certain age,

I'm afraid I'm not on the same page,

As many of my contemporaries

With their silver hair and replaced knees.

The secret of my cunning plan,

I'm married to a younger man.

He keeps me busy every day.

I love it when he gets that way!

I'm very happy can't you see,

To grow old, quite disgracefully.

Bring on hair dye and mascara,

Push up bra's, female Viagra.

Please don't give in and act your age,

Lift up, breathe in, strut, rant and rage.

My best advice to you would be,

To have a cunning plan like me.

Go find yourself a nice young man,

Be disgraceful whilst you can.

My husband tells me that most men's changing-rooms, do not have rear view mirrors. Could this be why most men think they look just fine?

Denial

Last week I went into the city

To buy a new dress, something pretty,

But I ended up not buying a dress,

Instead, headed home, in real distress.

I'd forgotten about that confidence killer,

The cursed and dreaded, changing room, rear view mirror.

I chose some clothes and counted them in,

With those plastic things, know what I mean.

Ready to try on the first new frock,

Was when I received a major shock.

There, right behind me, was this old crone.

I thought that I was there all alone.

What is she doing? Who can she be?

And then I realized, Good God, it's me.

The bra was grey, the knickers saggy,

The back, flabby and very baggy.

Whatever had happened to my bum?

Where had this ugly fat thing come from?

Why did my hair have a holey back?

Why were my arms all flabby and slack?

I left the shop in quite a hurry,

Buttons unfastened in my flurry.

I will not be going there again,

To play in the funny mirror game.

Of course, now I've had a cup of tea,

I have realized it was not me.

It must have been some ugly old crone,

Who'd escaped, from her retirement home.

A trick of light, an odd deflection,

Of some, old persons, sad reflection.

Someone should tell her to take more care.

I would never go out with a hole in my hair.

I went to the plastic surgeon

I went to see the plastic surgeon,

About a big spot on my cheek.

He said do you fancy a boob job?

I'm doing them on special next week

On being pregnant

I'm happy, I'm ecstatic. I'm as happy as can be.

The reason is I'm pregnant. It isn't hard to see.

I'm getting fatter every day. I'm fat as any pig.

Every day I look at me, I'm getting really big.

I'm so happy and I'm blooming. My life is very sweet.

Very soon I'll be so huge, I'll lose sight of my feet.

I just love it that I'm pregnant, I love it being so fat.

I look at all the thin girls; I used to look like that,

With flat, flat, tum' and skinny bum. I much prefer being me.

I'm happy. Oh! so happy. It's very clear to see,

That I'm plump, and very pregnant, a brand new mum to be.

Could you please excuse me I'm just dying for a pee!

We've all done it…….

The Diary

I thought I'd keep a diary, I thought it might be fun,

To keep a daily record of all the things I'd done.

I'd write it for my children to pass down through the years,

Soft, gentle words of wisdom to soothe away their fears;

A place they could refer to, to point them on their way,

Full, of wise and clever sayings, one for every day.

I bought my brand new diary. It had a little lock.

I hid it in the cupboard so nobody would mock

My many words of wisdom, recorded every night,

My sharp, and witty comments, my meaningful insights.

Each night before retiring, I'd write upon the page,

A literary masterpiece; not, merely, an adage.

I'd record my daily doings for posterity,

I had code names for the people, even one for me.

I did this for a complete week, did not miss a night,

Then I missed a couple. It was just an oversight

And then I missed a week, didn't write a single day.

Then, forgot to take it with me, when I went away.

Recently I found it. It was hidden in a sock,

A pencil in the binding, the key, still in the lock.

I looked back at the first week, but what were all those codes?

Who was J and X and what did P and Q denote?

Then I read the final entry for the 5th of May

Written in lonely splendour, "didn't do much today"

Not the words of wisdom I'd been seeking to impart

I guess I'm not a writer, instead I'll take up art!

Middle Aged Spread

Middle age spread arrives in the night.

It's just there in the morning. God, what a sight!

You went to bed feeling perfectly normal.

You didn't feel strange, or fat, or hormonal,

In the morning you woke up with this belly,

It's fat, it's flabby, it wobbles like jelly.

It hangs over your clothes in rolls at the side.

What used to be narrow is now very wide.

Oh! Where did it come from and what can I do?

No diet will shift it. We all know that's true.

So into tent dresses and old lady clothes,

Where did it come from? Nobody knows.

Dreaming by the sea

I love my old fella, and he loves me,

And as we sit dreaming here by the sea,

I think of all our long years together,

As time passes I wonder If ever,

He will, Oh So sweetly turn round to me,

And say, "My old sweetheart, please marry me."

I've longed for those words for so many years,

And many's the day I've shed bitter tears,

But I love this old fella. He loves me.

So, I'll keep on dreaming here by the sea.

I watched a baby on the beach

I watched a baby on the beach,

It did not know what to do.

It is a very frightening place

From a baby's point of view.

A baby's idea of water,

Is a warm and bubbly bath,

Not this wild, ferocious, boiling

Thing, beating its violent path,

Up the beach to where baby

Sits, not knowing what to do.

A beach is a very frightening place

From a baby's point of view.

Mothers Day

Watch my lips. Pay attention. Hear what I say.

I don't want a steam mop for my Mother's Day.

The main reason being that washing the floor,

Modern steam mop, or not, it's still quite a chore.

Nor do I desire the latest new iron,

A drill, or even a microwave oven,

A brand new duster, a fancy bread baker,

A toilet brush or toasted sandwich maker.

I do not want a kit for some home brewed beer,

Or, a gift-voucher for some D.I.Y. gear.

I can still remember what happened last year.

(The scars are fading where they sewed back my ear.)

Something made by the kids with card, string, and glue,

With pink wobbly writing saying "Mum, we love you."

I'd like that so much, but it might make me cry,

Or, you think of something. Please, give it a try.

If you're going to spend just a little more,

How about a fabulous foot pedicure?

Or, may-be, a day in a luxury spa?

Perhaps that is going a little too far.

Now, where are you going? Pray, what's in that box?

What's that long, thin object going back to the shops?

Can't begin to imagine what it might be.

I do hope that it was a steam mop for me.

In almost all department stores in the UK there is

a section devoted to beige clothes for the timid

and the elderly.

They are generally made from polyester with

extra fabric in the bum and elasticized waists.

They are almost always too short or too long

They have big pockets on the hips for your hanky.

They are often accompanied by blouses made

from curtain fabric

Beige clothes

Clearly, as a woman of a certain age,

I'm supposed to give up sex and dress in beige.

Although I may admit to a few beige clothes,

Believe me ladies that's as far as it goes.

I think that the source of my frivolity,

Could well be my daily dose of HRT.

Either that, or medicinal glass of wine,

I've been known to indulge in from time to time,

Or perhaps the odd little tot of whisky.

It's well understood that it keeps you frisky.

Or sometimes a small glass or three of brandy,

It's good for your heart. I'm feeling quite dandy!

On reflection I think I'll buy some red clothes,

And throw out the beige. I'm not ready for those!

I have a friend who said to her husband,

"Next time I have a phone, I would like one with

a camera."

He said,

"Your phone has a camera!!!!"

Getting Mobile

I thought I'd join the modern world

And buy me a smart mobile phone.

I'd talk to people on the bus

And tell them I'd soon be back home.

I went to the mobile phone shop.

I told them I wanted a phone.

But they blinded me with science,

Talked of, polyphonic ring tones.

They asked, "Do you want a camera?"

I said, "No. Why would I want that?"

I've got my faithful old Brownie.

I showed them my holiday snaps.

I decided to go Virgin,

(Richard Branson's a lovely man.)

I liked the shape and the colour,

And the new pre-paid payment plan.

It's got lots of buttons and lights

And it plays a loud jingly tune.

If I really study the manual,

I'll be able to answer it soon.

Isn't the menopause fun?

As I sat in the garden one fine day,

I thought of something I really must say

To you ladies who are a certain age,

For you, I will write it upon this page.

Isn't the menopause fun?

Don't you enjoy all the aches and the pains,

The grey thinning hair, the varicose veins?

It was always lovely to be desired,

Now I'm too busy, too hot or too tired.

At least twenty times, by day and by night,

I experience, to my great delight,

A sudden, unwelcome and searing heat,

That travels from my face through to my feet.

My clothes, I must choose now, with extra care,

Allowing their removal, layer by layer,

As the room suddenly becomes so hot

I am reduced to a pink, sweaty, spot.

Isn't the menopause fun?

HRT, once the cure for all our ills,

Is now on the bad list of don't take pills.

So it's back to the sweats and sleepless nights,

The memory loss and those mood swing fights.

I did not believe it when I was told,

That I'd quite look forward to being old;

To be able to sit in summer sun,

Without sweat, running down the crack in my bum.

All good things must come to an end they say,

It can't be long now, almost any day,

And the bloody thing might just go away.

And then at last I'll look back and I'll say

Wasn't the menopause fun?

Having vacuumed up a huge web I returned to

find myself confronted by a giant Huntsman

spider.

It tried to stare me down.

Never hit a huntsman with a fly-swat.

They explode.

Thedric the Thpider

I'm Thedric and I am a thpider ,

Thuperior, thexthy and thtrong.

I live with my wife and kiddieth

Under a big thhelf in Hong Kong.

My thpidery wife ith called Thuthan,

Her webth are a delicate art.

Thhe won many prithes for thpinning

At our Thivic Thentre for Art.

Weve got thixth thpidery children,

Their ageth are thix to thixteen.

Three boyth, two girlth and another,

Who'th thomehow,thomewhere in between.

We all thtrive very hard for our living,

We all thpin from morning to night,

Tho pleathe don't think we are horrid

And thcream, if we hove, into thight.

Pleathe don't thquath uth, or thpray uth,

That would be tho terribly wrong,

'Coth I'm Thedric, thuperman thpider,

thuperior,thexy and thtrong.

.

The Nosey Neighbour

I live at number 22,

My house, it is small and cosy.

My only problem living here,

Is, my neighbours think I'm nosey.

I've no idea why they think that,

But they watch me all the day long.

I don't know why they all do that,

I have not done anything wrong.

I am trying to be helpful,

And to keep a kind, friendly eye,

On all of my neighbour's doings.

They all know that I do not pry

Into their odd little secrets.

They just know they are safe with me.

Even though I've written them down,

They're quite safe under lock and key.

The other day from 8 to 9

Whilst idly glancing through my nets,

I saw my neighbour running late,

(She now works at the local vets.)

It was almost quarter past nine,

When she, at last left in her car.

So, I phoned the vet to tell him.

It's just as well it's not too far.

The man at number 17,

 (I found out that his name is Dave.)

Each day as he is passing by,

Always gives me this funny wave.

Strange! He's only got two fingers.

I find it really very sad.

One day I did it back to him

He became incredibly mad.

And then the folks at 24

Left their old dog out, in the yard.

So, I poked it with big a stick

To start it barking really hard.

Then I telephoned the ranger

To make complaint about the noise.

I said, "It does it all the time,

And also chases little boys."

My dear landlord, he has told me

That he will not renew my lease.

But I've fixed him. I've dobbed him in,

He is now helping the police

With their own investigation,

Into my last fictitious crime.

The least he will get is probation.

He will most probably do time.

I'm just such a helpful person.

I can't help it that I'm so nice.

Perhaps, if you'd like to know me,

You will listen to my advice.

If you know of a vacant house,

Then please do yourself a favour,

Tell me exactly where it is,

And I could be your new neighbour

Elastic Waistbands

Elastic waist bands

Are wonderful things.

They let me be fat,

But make me feel thin.

Tell me what you see

I'm tired of being a spinster,

I'm just fed up not being wed.

I'm so sick of lonely nights

In my little, single bed.

So tell me fortune teller,

Tell me what it is you see.

In your magic, crystal ball,

Is there a good man for me?

I'd like him to be handsome,

I'd prefer him to be tall,

But small and fat and ugly

Is better than none at all.

I'd like him to be wealthy

And head a corporation,

But unemployed will do,

Such is my desperation.

He will need to have a house,

With pink roses round the door.

Or, even just a unit,

On the first or second floor.

He ought to drive a sports car

That converts to open top.

At least his unit must be

On a road, with a bus stop.

I'd prefer him well endowed,

To give me lots of pleasure.

But, if he's not? Oh well!

Nobody's going to measure.

So, tell me fortune teller,

Tell me what it is you see.

When you search your crystal ball,

Do you see a man for me?

My friend Carol and I went shopping. My husband asked me if I had bought anything. I told him I'd bought a dress.

He said," Carol bought a dress?'

I said, "No, I'd bought a dress."

He said, "but you've got a dress".

Says it all really!

The Thrifty Wife

I must say I'm really extremely surprised

 How quickly the credit card bills have arrived.

It seems no time at all since the last one came.

What do you mean? " The amount will be the same

As the last one, because we've spent no money."

Sorry to say, It's confession time honey.

I'm afraid that I have spent a small amount.

No I'm not sure how much. I just didn't count.

Why don't you sit down? Let me pour you a drink.

I'll try to remember, I need time to think.

The sales all were on in the top fashion shops,

But don't worry honey 'cos I saved you lots.

I saved over a hundred on my new shoes,

An absolute bargain, 'cos they're Jimmy Choos.

The heels are too high, and they're a size too small,

But at that price cost almost nothing at all

And then, of course, to match, I needed a dress.

I tried on dozens with no sign of success,

Until I found this really fabulous gown,

It's beautiful and they had marked it right down.

I saved you at least a hundred and fifty.

You must be proud that I'm being so thrifty.

It's a bit too small, I will need to diet.

By Christmas I should be able to try it.

But, the things that saved you the greatest money,

Were my new handbags, you'll just love them honey.

They're made from the softest Italian leather.

With a choice of two, I didn't know whether

To go for the black one, or the Champaign beige.

Pale, soft colours are in; they're the latest craze.

So, I just bought them both for the price of one,

I knew you'd be pleased and I had so much fun.

To you it might seem like a lot of money

But, I've got this great little theory honey.

If I buy a garment and wear it just once,

Well everyone knows that's sheer extravagance.

But, instead if I use it every day,

The way that I use my handbag, you might say,

Then the more I use it the cheaper it gets.

So, if I use it often, wear it to death,

Each time that I use it, it's costing you less.

It's not very long 'til it's nearly worthless.

So, that after, lets say, just a week or two

I can throw it away and buy something new.

Honey, are you sure that you're feeling OK?

Your face has become a quite strange shade of grey.

Lie back, put your feet up, I'll top up your drink.

You're breathing is odd and your eyes are quite pink.

Perhaps what you need is a good holiday.

We'll pay for it out of the money I've saved.

Moving South

Standing in front of the mirror, I just can't believe that it's me.

Now and then I catch a glimpse of the person that I used to be.

But the hair is a different colour, short and really quite thin,

As for the figure, it's bigger. I don't know just where to begin.

The overall shape is the same, a body, a head and a mouth,

But the problem is that it's moved. It's now six inches further

south.

The boobs are most certainly lower .The waist is almost not there,

The bum now is flatter but fatter it really is most unfair.

Now if this rapid descent keeps on going, even as we speak,

My fat knees will be joining my ankles by the end of the week.

I thought that I might reverse things by trying to stand on my

head,

I just got fat shoulders and heartburn, not good it has to be said.

Then I found the perfect answer. I threw all the long mirrors out.

Now my face is all that I see. Who cares if my body is stout?

It's the estrogen in the water

If you are taking the pill, or maybe HRT,

You are passing out estrogen every time you pee.

It goes into our rivers and finally to sea,

Where, the fishes take it in for breakfast, lunch and tea.

It's having dire effects on their sexuality,

They do not know any more if they are he or she.

"So?" you say," there only fish," but no, apparently

Moving up the food chain, it's affecting you and me.

It's not just the fish you see suffering from delusion,

Many humans too are experiencing confusion.

Maybe you have seen my friend? She's very tall and thin.

You would even be forgiven for thinking that her 's a him

She has a hairy top lip and quite a stubbly chin,

She wears suits and shirts and ties and looks quite masculine.

Adding more confusion to this modern gender mess,

She has a hairy boyfriend who sometimes wears a dress.

Modern names as well are quite often trans-gender.

It looks as though we are really trying to send a

Message to the world, that we're not certain who we are.

All we can do is guess using sexual radar.

Scientists, say it's the estrogen in the waters

That 's causing all our sons to change into our daughters.

So if you are on the pill or even HRT,

Please consider what you're doing every time you pee.

Old Age Sucks

I'm old and I'm ugly

And nobody cares.

I can't stand for long and

I struggle with stairs.

Dressing in the morning,

Well that's just an art.

I am frightened to sneeze,

It might make me fart.

I can't see my watch,

The numbers are smaller.

I can't reach top shelves,

I used to be taller.

My boobs which were lovely

Now are much flatter.

My tiny trim waist,

Well that's much, much fatter.

My nose has grown long.

And my ears now have flaps.

I'm wrinkled and baggy.

I need lots of naps.

Repeating my stories,

Has made me a bore.

And my friends three doors down,

They tell me I snore.

I don't like old age,

I don't like it at all.

I don't like false teeth.

I don't like being small.

I liked being young

It has to be said.

But look on the bright side,

I'll soon be quite dead!

Dream on!

When I was young and feeling flirty,

Middle age began at thirty.

But now I'm thirty, seems to me,

It might begin at forty three.

But by then, I am almost sure,

It will begin at fifty four.

I guess no-one will disagree,

I'm pushing it at 63!

When you were small

Can you recall when you were small?

And, all the world was really tall.

You'd eat and sleep and poop and bawl,

Until, the day that you could crawl.

And at last you start to toddle.

That walking lark, just a doddle!

Your world was ankles, calves and knees,

Big bottom drawers, and cats to tease.

Your main desire, just to explore,

Was always thwarted that's for sure.

Harnesses, reins, playpens and prams.

If it was good, it had a ban.

My Mummy's hand was very high,

Somewhere up there beside the sky.

And even tho' I'd try and try

I couldn't keep up and I'd cry.

So……

Do you recall when you were small?

 It was crap wasn't it?

Most women of a certain age have experienced

feelings of becoming inaudible and invisible.

Excuse me. I'm talking to you…….

Fading Away

It seems in my fifties that I'm fading away.

People no longer see me or hear what I say.

For now all that they see is the hair going grey,

And believe that the brain's also wasting away.

Although no longer young I am not really old.

Don't assume that my hot blood is now running cold.

The lessons that I've learned are worth their weight in gold.

The life story to come yet is still to be told,

I'm no longer as handsome or nimble as you.

Mirrors do not reflect an enjoyable view.

But don't lock me in limbo with nothing to do.

Don't dismiss what I say and don't ever pooh pooh

My thoughts and opinions. I'm much wiser than you.

Although the technologies and systems are new,

I learned to e-mail and text without much ado

And there are things at which I am better than you.

I understand grammar, long multiplication,

I can write proper letters, hold conversation,

I also belonged to the drugs generation.

So, what we deserve is some appreciation

For us folk in our fifties; just think of the Stones,

They're still rocking away on their fragile old bones.

So now in my mid life you must hear what I say.

I've dyed my hair orange. I just won't fade away.

I have lots to contribute, on that I insist,

I won't spiral down into that dark grey abyss

So, a bit of respect from you won't go amiss.

But, most of all you youngsters, just remember this

Carefree youth does not last and one day you will know

What it's like to be older and past that first glow;

No longer a person, a mere ghost, a shadow,

Then I'll sit and I'll weep because I told you so.

Do you, like me, always choose the wrong

Super-market queue?

Why I'm on probation

The judge, he put me on probation.

Saying there was some provocation.

I did not really mean to do it.

It was in my hand, I just threw it.

I'm certain that if I just explain,

You will sympathise. You'd do the same.

I don't know if this happens to you.

I speak of the super-market queue.

No matter whichever one I choose,

I'm always behind the person whose

Mind is not upon the job.

The one who is the perfect picker

Of, the item without a sticker.

The one who stands up there in a dream,

Idly flicking, through a magazine.

They just never seem to have the thought,

"I will need to pay for what I've bought."

So when the check out chick is all done,

And has packed the items one by one,

They replace the magazine, well thumbed,

Back onto the shelf, and looking stunned

They dive deep into a huge hand bag.

But first, they glare at the growing queue,

As tho' it's something to do with you

That they've to pay for the goods they've bought.

It's never their fault. Perish the thought.

As we wait and the queue gets longer,

This woman starts to rake among her

Worldly goods.

And from the various zippered pockets,

Out come lipstick, tissues, pens dockets,

And then at last a smile she flashes.

We hold our breath. She waves her glasses.

The long queue by now is fifteen deep.

At least one of them is fast asleep.

At last, at last, she finds her money.

But, big mistake, she finds it funny.

So, if you see across the nation,

On every single TV station,

That, Caucasian woman, fifty two,

A bit overweight, grey, permed hairdo,

Without apparent provocation,

But, with, it seems, the approbation

Of the angry super-market queue,

Picked up a roasted chicken and threw

It hard at an innocent young Mum,

Whacking her, squarely, across the bum.

Don't be surprised when you see it's me,

Because I am very rapidly,

Becoming the kind of person who,

Attacks, other people in the queue.

The judge he put me on probation.

Saying there was some provocation

What if?

I can remember who I am. I can't remember why.

Perhaps it will just come to me sometime before I die.

Being daughter, wife and mother twenty four hours a day,

Leaves little time for self- indulgence, even, less for play.

The great career I'd promised me when all the kids left home,

Was suddenly, too much like work, enthusiasm gone.

My little talent seemed too small for me to make my mark.

I'd be content with what I'd done, I didn't have the heart

To use my tiny talent, to develop it with glee,

To stop being daughter, wife and Mum, instead try just being me.

Perhaps I no longer exist. What if I'm just not there?

What if without the status names I'm just a puff of air?

What if I reach the pearly gates and God won't let me in?

What if neglecting our talent is deemed a mortal sin?

What if God says the job I did really was essential,

But, what about all the rest? Fulfilling my potential.

What if he says I wasn't born so I could pick and choose?

Which bits of life I could neglect and which bits I would use?

So look out world, here I come and I will remember why

I am here, and just who I am. I'm aiming for the sky.

Divorce

I have it from a reliable source,

Told in confidence, of course

The most common reason for divorce,

Is marriage

The very best thing about a secret is the

telling of it to someone else!

The Secret

(With apologies to anyone called Sue)

Have you heard the latest news about that scrubber Sue?

Bearing it in mind of course, it might just not be true.

Mary told Miranda, and Miranda she told Pru.

Pru told me and Nancy and so now I'll just tell you.

All this is in confidence. I promised not to tell,

You know I never gossip and so it's just as well

That you can keep a secret. I know its safe with you.

Like me, you just won't tell if you give your word not to.

I know you are as honest as anyone can be.

I know you are trustworthy. You are a lot like me.

Because, I can keep a secret, just as well as you.

But have you heard the latest about that scrubber Sue?

World's most elegant bag lady

When I'm old I plan to be

The world's most elegant, bag lady.

I'll only sleep in Harrods doorway,

I shoplift there 'most every Tuesday.

I especially like their marron glace,

They're frightfully tasty and awfully classy.

Even my bags will be fantastic,

Louis Vuitton, not nasty plastic.

After all, one's secret plan

Must be to be the best one can.

So when I'm old I plan to be

The world's most elegant, bag lady.

When I drink, I'll drink champagne.

Sparkling wine is not the same.

I plan to wear my Jimmy Choo shoes,

Whilst raking the bins at Waterloo.

I'll wear my furs. They won't be fake,

Whilst I first demand, and then partake

Of Earl Grey tea and chocolate cake,

Meanwhile, charming, my handsome date.

Only the best will do you see

For the world's most elegant, bag lady.

I'll pretend I have an account with Coutts,

That, the Queen and I are in cahoots.

And at Harvey Nicholls perfume stand,

I'll spray their perfumes on my hand,

So that if I die one cold, cold night,

They'll say, "She was a splendid sight."

Wrapped in furs and smelling sweet,

Designer, shoes, upon her feet.

They'll say I really have to be,

The world's, most elegant, bag lady.

I will not even die the poor way.

Not I, I'll die in Harrods doorway!

Gordon the Warden

Where I now live, in a retirement home,

There's nothing to do and no-one to 'phone.

I'm not really sure where my life has gone.

I fantasize lots, sitting on my own.

My light switches all have extra cord on,

So, if I fall, I can call the warden.

He's a handsome hunk. His name is Gordon.

All the old ladies fancy the Warden.

So, I pull his cord whenever I can.

It's an easy way to summon a man.

The last time I called him to visit me,

I flirted with him quite outrageously.

I clicked my false teeth so seductively.

I showed him the scar on my replaced knee.

I wiggled my toes provocatively

I hoped he'd ignore the aroma of pee

I offered to show him my magic trick,

Involving, my trusted, old, walking stick.

But, he rapidly backed towards the door.

Then, Gordon, the Warden; He was no more.

Oh Well! I suppose it's time for my tea.

I'll set out my tray. I'll watch some TV.

I'll take all my pills, It's true what they say,

That's enough excitement for just one day.

I'll go to my bed, dream of my Gordon,

And have my wicked way with the Warden.

Temptation

It's almost 2am in the morning.

I awake with a burning desire.

I'm so full of lust, I think I might bust.

Only one thing will put out the fire.

What I need is a dark chocolate Tim Tam.

What I need is to lick its' dark coat.

What I need is to feel its' soft texture,

As it melts, down the back of my throat.

I jump out of my bed in my nightie.

I fly swiftly through the sleeping house,

My instinct tells me where I'm going,

To the fridge, like an Exocet mouse.

But, the shelf in the fridge is quite empty,

Except, for a wrapper; torn. Not a

Tim Tam in sight, not a crumb, of delight.

All the Tim Tams appear to have gone.

On the wrapper a bright yellow post-it,

From my husband, still sleeping in bed.

Those words I will remember forever,

And, the words that my dear husband said?

Dearest wife, I thought you might be tempted.

I just thought you might have to give in,

So, I've eaten the dark chocolate Tim Tams

From your loving and full husband, Jim.

So, that's the end of the poetry,

That's the end of the book.

 If you like what you see,

Then please contact me.

Address next page if you look.

If you wish to contact
the author regarding
poetry readings, book or
CD sales please
E-mail

ellie-art@hotmail.com